FEMME FATALE

BIOGRAPHY

Polly was born in Sussex and at 18, moved to London to train as an actor at the Royal Academy of Dramatic Art. She quickly realised that most of the roles for women were shit, and decided to write some plays where they got more of the fun stuff. She became a member of the Royal Court Young Writers programme, who produced her short play **Trying It On** (also adapted for BBC TV) and where she met Nathan Evans, the director of Femme Fatale.

Her plays include: **Damage Control** for Playground Theatre, **Reflections** for BYMT at Saddlers' Wells, **Somewhere In England**, produced by Eastern Angles, **Manchester Sound: The Massacre**, produced by Manchester Library Theatre, nominated for a Manchester Theatre Award, **The Power**, short-listed for the Nick Darke Award, **Bright**, produced by Soho Theatre, **Trying It On** produced by Royal Court Theatre Upstairs and adapted for TV for BBC Fiction Lab, **Loaded**, awarded a Peggy Ramsay Foundation bursary, produced by Yvonne Arnaud Theatre, **The Pinball Master**, for the National Theatre Studio and Birmingham Rep, **Stormin' Jack Norman**, produced by Menagerie TC, at Theatre 503 in London and The Roxy Theatre in Edmonton, Canada, **Swedish Rustic**, produced at BAC, **Fierce**: Canadian tour, **Andy & Edie**, produced by Fireraisers Theatre Company, toured the UK, nominated for a Total Theatre Award, **Atomic**, produced by Atomic Productions at Latitude Festival.

She has been Writer-On-Attachment for Birmingham Rep, Theatre Absolute and Theatre Royal Margate. Polly co-founded Fireraisers Theatre Company, which The Guardian called 'one of the great hopes of British Theatre'.

A million years ago, she was a style journalist for i-D magazine, The Evening Standard and various others. And for a while, she worked as 'Door Whore' Polly Vinyl at the Royal Vauxhall Tavern.

She lives in East London with her wonderful husband, Khobir Icarus Newton Wiseman-Goldstein.

praise for Polly Wisemann

'Wiseman's writing sears and burns'
The Guardian

'Wiseman's challenging and sensitive play is perfectly pitched'
The Stage

praise for Femme Fatale

'With its strong feminist theme, Femme Fatale—directed by Nathan Evans—is of the moment.
Both Wiseman and Olivia are quite brilliant'
Jeff Prestridge, Close-Up Culture

'Wow that was brilliant!'
Nic Connaughton, Head of Theatre at The Pleasance

FEMME FATALE

Polly Wiseman

Published by Inkandescent, 2019

Text Copyright © 2019 Polly Wiseman

Photography and Design Copyright © 2019 Justin David

Polly Wiseman has asserted her right under the Copyright, Designs and Patents Act 1988 to be identified as the author of this work.

All rights reserved. No part of this publication may be reproduced, stored in a retrieval system, or transmitted in any form or by any means, electronic, mechanical, photocopying, recording or otherwise, without the prior permission of the publisher.

While every precaution has been taken in the preparation of this book, the publisher assumes no responsibilities for errors or omissions, or for damages resulting from the information contained herein.

ISBN 978-1-912620-06-7 (paperback)

1 3 5 7 9 10 8 6 4 2

www.inkandescent.co.uk

For my niece, Ava Harvey.
Go out and kick ass. But don't shoot anybody

INTRODUCTION

It's still really hard, as a woman, to live an unconventional life and be celebrated for it. I think it's high time that changed—which is why I wanted to write about Teutonic junkie Nico and 'feminazi assassin' Valerie Solanas. Both revolutionaries, in their different ways, their legacy has been all but ignored in favour of more compliant and prettily-packaged women. But thirty years after they both died, their work continues to inspire artists and activists working today.

As singer with The Velvet Underground, Nico exuded Ice Maiden cool. But she grew to hate her glamorous blond image and, in her solo career, dyed her hair brown, became a heroin addict and pioneered a whole new genre of music as the 'Godmother of Goth'. Clearly, there were dark roots beneath the shiny blond surface. Valerie Solanas is remembered (when she ever is) as the angry psycho who shot Andy Warhol, but she was an influential second wave feminist. When I read her 1968 SCUM Manifesto—Society for Cutting Up Men—I found it both hilarious and utterly relevant. Realising Valerie and Nico had been in the same Warhol movie (I, A Man), an idea started to form: what would happen if I put these two uncompromising characters in a room together? As the 2017/18 revelations of sexual abuse in Hollywood came to light, I started to consider Valerie's shooting of Andy Warhol as an early #Times Up moment. The time seemed ripe for a reimagining of two female pop culture icons, battling for control of their own destinies.

As two contrasting versions of womanhood—the blond, compliant 60s chick and the angry, androgynous activist—they embody different ways of negotiating a man's world as a woman.

The fact that they had such different accents (American/German), tempos and speech patterns, made them a lot of fun to write. Despite their contrasting personalities, they have one thing in common: they gave precisely zero fucks—and a hundred years since women got the vote, that's still a punishable offence. Recent world events remind us we're still fighting for control of our stories and our bodies.

But Femme Fatale is a comedy, albeit a dark and unconventional one. Both these women were outsiders, coping with mental illness, poverty, addiction, abuse and—in Valerie's case—homelessness, begging and sex work; they used gallows humour as a survival tactic. And it's a cabaret-play because I want the characters to be able to interact directly with a modern audience. Alongside the show, we're making a new feminist Manifesto for 2019 and we'd love our audiences and online friends to contribute to it. Use the hashtag #SCUM2019 on Twitter and Instagram, or go to our website www.fireraisers.org.uk to have your say. Thank you!

Polly Wiseman, August 2019

Sophie Olivia as Valerie Solanas, photographed by Justin David

Valerie Solanas: Schizo dyke or icon of alienation?

'Life in this society being, at best, an utter bore and no aspect of society being at all relevant to women, there remains to civic-minded, thrill-seeking females only to overthrow the government, eliminate the money system, institute complete automation, and destroy the male sex.'
Valerie Solanas, SCUM Manifesto intro, 1967

Valerie Solanas didn't have the best start in life. Growing up in a working class home in 1940s New Jersey, she was abused by her alcoholic father and had given birth to two children by the time she was fifteen—one by a married sailor on leave, the other by her own father. When her parents divorced soon after, she lived first with her mother and new stepfather before being sent to live with her alcoholic grandfather. At a time of conformity and conservatism in 1950s America, Valerie provocatively came out as a lesbian while at high school, suffering prejudice and extreme bullying as a consequence. Somehow she managed to enrol at the University of Maryland, graduating as a psychology major.

The cumulative trauma of her young life—poverty, abuse, neglect, bullying—left her alienated and resentful, distrustful of relationships and angry at the world as she knew it. Having endured the unrelenting inhumanity of the world around her, she decided that she could never ever participate in it. And in the mid-1960s she started writing the tirade that would become the SCUM manifesto.

Valerie was not a prolific writer and virtually nothing she wrote was published. Her play *Up Your Ass* was recently performed for the first time, having been lost for decades; despite her uncompromising world view, she was able—in 1966—to write *A Young Girl's Primer on How to Attain the Leisure Class* for Cavalier, a 'gentleman's magazine'. The SCUM manifesto remains the document that defines her.

The introduction quoted above sets the tone, arguing that men have ruined the world, and that it is up to women to fix it. She is incandescent about the structural violence inflicted on women by men and makes it clear that there is no middle ground 'SCUM wants to destroy the system, not attain certain rights within it.' The bulk of the manifesto is a long list of critiques of the male sex and concludes that the elimination of the male sex is a moral imperative.

Was the entire manifesto to be taken literally? More likely Valerie's intention was to provoke by overstatement. It has often been compared to Jonathan Swift's *A Modest Proposal*, a political satire that suggested that the Irish Famine could be resolved by feeding unwanted babies to the pigs. The SCUM manifesto is written with passion but also wit. It is utterly uncompromising, relevant and prescient, a call to arms that is hard to ignore.

Unsurprisingly, Valerie fitted well into the world of outcasts and freaks that gravitated to Andy Warhol's Factory, introduced by drag queen and sometime roommate Candy Darling. Hoping that Andy would produce her play *Up Your Ass*, she entrusted him with her only typescript copy. When he claimed to have lost it, she snapped. On 3 June 1968 she returned to The Factory, pulled a handgun from her bag and fired three shots at Warhol as he chatted on the phone. Two missed but the third pierced several vital organs. As Andy was rushed to hospital, Valerie ran out of the building and later surrendered to a traffic cop in Times Square.

Famous overnight, many would-be feminist allies and radical groups supported her cause but over time she rebuffed them all, seeing them no less than Warhol as opportunists out to appropriate her work. Despite a diagnosis of paranoid schizophrenia, she received a three year custodial sentence, served in various brutal prisons and hospitals for the criminally insane. Life after prison was even worse than before, marked by loneliness and extreme hardship—although she did live for two years, seemingly happily, with a male partner—until her illness destroyed this relationship. She spent much of the 1970s revising the *SCUM Manifesto* and working on an autobiography, but poverty and illness steadily robbed her of lucidity and eventually sent her onto the streets. She died of pneumonia in 1988 in a welfare hotel in San Francisco.

Valerie Solanas has had an afterlife of sorts: in several plays, the film *I Shot Andy Warhol*, a Velvet Underground song and on television, where she was played by Lena Dunham in an episode of *American Horror Story*. But mostly she is remembered as the 'schizo dyke' who gained her 15 minutes of fame when she shot Andy Warhol. What she was, in the end, was a singular voice at odds with the world, angry, passionate and unafraid. The SCUM manifesto expresses her uncontainable disgust at the extent and depth of misogyny. Better to remember her as an icon of alienation?

Polly Wiseman as Nico, photographed by Justin David

Nico: From 60s sex symbol to the Godmother of Goth

In 1954 at a Berlin fashion show photographer Herbert Tobias met a tall, skinny teenager with big eyes, sensuous lips and chiselled features. Her name was Christa Päffgen. Recognising her potential as a model, he suggested that she change her name to something snappier and more memorable. Nico was born that day— a name she would keep for the rest of her life.

Born in Cologne in 1938, Nico at first glance is the antithesis of Valerie Solanas. Beautiful, blond, successful, Warhol Superstar —a true 1960s icon. But her real story is far darker and much more interesting. Her mother was a skilled dressmaker, and her father—a soldier in Hitler's Third Reich—vanished in unexplained circumstances after a crippling head wound. Fatherless (and perfectly mirroring Valerie's young life) she too was sent to live with her grandparents, this time in a small town fifty miles from Berlin, where she loved to play in the graveyard. This rural idyll ended abruptly when the family moved to the capital after the war. Berlin in 1946 was still in ruins, those who had survived the bombing still gaunt and hungry. Nico later recalled it as 'a desert of bricks… it is something that hides behind my lyrics like scenery'. She found work with her mother in a department store, where she was able to do some rudimentary modelling on the side. Aged 14—the same age that Valerie bore her first child—Christa was raped by an American sergeant. Her evidence resulted in the man's conviction.

A year later she met Herbert Tobias and Nico's life began. Soon she was a successful model working for Elle, Vogue and Chanel, travelling across Europe in style and meeting the beau monde. Federico Fellini gave her a small part in *La Dolce Vita* and this led to other film offers. But with a growing sense of her own worth, she resented being manipulated and used by others; she wanted to be in control of her own destiny. She determined to become a singer.

A brief affair with Bob Dylan resulted in his song about her

I'll Keep It with Mine. Another affair with actor Alain Delon resulted in a son Ari. Brian Jones of the Rolling Stones arranged her first recording session in London, although the record flopped. Later in 1964 she was introduced to Andy Warhol in his New York Factory, where the house band was The Velvet Underground, part of his mixed-media happening *The Exploding Plastic Inevitable.* Warhol was about to produce the Velvet's iconic 'Yellow Banana' album and, to the consternation of front men Lou Reed and John Cale, decided that Nico would become their 'chanteuse'. Nico's distinctive deadpan vocals feature on three tracks including *Femme Fatale. The Velvet Underground & Nico* is ranked at number thirteen on Rolling Stone magazine's list of the '500 Greatest Albums of All Time'.

Underestimated as a creative force, mistreated by countless lovers, and reduced to a pretty puppet by a series of male songwriters, it's not hard to imagine why Nico came to despise her bewitching appearance. She left the Velvets and embarked on a solo career with her album *Chelsea Girls.* Over time she abandoned her ice-queen beauty, put on weight and let her hair return to its natural brunette. She recalled 'My life started after my experience with the Velvet Underground'. By now she was a heroin user, having graduated from amphetamines. Her 1969 follow up album *The Marble Index* was a dramatic departure that revealed a new doom-laden gothic persona characterised by dark vocals, often impenetrable lyrics and ghostly harmonium. With a growing drug dependency and self-destructive private life, her career dwindled. In the 70s she made seven films in France with her then partner Philippe Garrel, also appearing at various festivals around Europe. In 1978 Nico briefly toured as supporting act for Siouxsie and the Banshees, one of many post-punk bands who namechecked her. Becoming a cult figure for a new generation, the 'Godmother of Goth' embarked on a relentless touring schedule that took her all over Europe and beyond—where audience reaction ranged from reverence to open hostility.

In her final years, she was based in Manchester and London,

where she lived for a while with the punk-poet John Cooper Clark. She made heroic attempts in the late 1980s to turn her life around, switching from heroin to methadone, trading junk food and gothic lethargy for organics and regular exercise. In 1988, while cycling on holiday in her beloved Ibiza, she had a minor heart attack, fell from her bike and hit her head on a rock. She died the same evening.

Now recognised as the original goth rocker, Nico's albums are demanding and bleak, but map a singular and starkly powerful vision that has become more influential with age.

Characters:

Nico (female, German, 30s, Warhol Superstar)
Valerie Solanas (female, American, 30s, radical feminist)

Setting:
Room 546, The Chelsea Hotel, New York, 1967 – and other time periods…

Cast:

An earlier draft of *Femme Fatale* premiered at Wilton's Music Hall, London in July 2018 with the following cast:

Nico	Polly Wiseman
Valerie	Sophie Olivia

The current draft of *Femme Fatale* premiered at Kino Theatr, St Leonards-on-Sea in September 2019, before touring to Leaf Hall (Eastbourne), Depot (Lewes), Latest Music Bar (Brighton) and running at Omnibus Theatre, London with the following cast:

Nico	Polly Wiseman
Valerie	Sophie Olivia
Director	Nathan Evans
Producer	Fireraisers
Associate producer	Elise Phillips
Lighting designer	Sophie Bailey
Stage designer	Sally Hardcastle
Sound & Video design	Nathan Evans & Sophie Bailey
Stage manager	Olivia Presto
Publicist	Flavia Fraser-Cannon
Publicity photos & design	Justin David

Sophie Olivia (Valerie Solanas) Sophie's favourite roles in theatre include: Beatrice (Much Ado About Nothing), Anna Labia (Saucy Jack and the Space Vixens), Julia (Duchess of Malfi) and Slag (I Licked a Slag's Deodorant) She has most recently worked at the TRSE, Park Theatre, Arcola and the ORL.

Nathan Evans (director) Nathan is a writer, director and performer whose work in theatre and film has been funded by the Arts Council, toured by the British Council, broadcast on Channel 4, archived by the British Film Institute and produced at venues including Soho Theatre, Southbank Centre, ICA, BAC and Latitude Festival. *www.nathanevans.co.uk*

Fireraisers (producer) Fireraisers presents extraordinary theatre in unexpected places and illuminates the stories of outsider women. They have presented co-productions with Soho Theatre, Birmingham Rep, Hampstead Theatre and shows in unusual locations around the UK. *www.fireraisers.org.uk*

Elise Phillips (associate producer) Elise has over fifteen years of producing and management experience. She works with independent artists, NPOs and large organisations, specialising in dance but also across art forms, particularly in community arts engagement. She's based in Brighton. *www.elisephillipsdance.co.uk*

Sophie Bailey (lighting designer) Sophie graduated from Liverpool Institute of Performing Arts with a 1st Class BA Honours in Theatre and Performance Technology. She was recipient of the Michael Northen Award for 2018. Credits include: *Moon Dances* (Pegasus Theatre), *Rainbow Connection* (Royal Court Liverpool). *www.sophiebaileydesign.co.uk*

Sally Hardcastle (stage designer) Sally is based in London and Essex. Since graduating with a degree in Theatre Design from Rose Bruford College she has worked with organisations including Wild Rumpus, The Bread and Roses and The Gate Theatre. She is co-founder and resident designer of new company Matipo. *www.sallyhardcastle.com*

Olivia Presto (stage manager) Olivia is a stage manager from Manchester. She studied Drama and Theatre Practice at the University of Hull. After graduating, she took part in a work place internship with the Royal Shakespeare Company. Credits include: Wonderhouse Theatre's *Mydidae* and Hull UK City of Culture project *Weathered Estates*.

Flavia Fraser-Cannon (publicist) Flavia has been an account manager at Mobius Industries—who work with the most exciting and inventive companies, venues and artists in theatre, dance and comedy—since 2016. She's also worked with ATG, Theatre503 and Finger in the Pie cabaret. *www.mobiusindustries.com*

Justin David (publicity designer) Justin lives and works in London. He studied BA Graphic Communication at the University of Northampton and MA Creative and Life Writing at Goldsmiths. His photographs have appeared in magazines including Attitude and Time Out, his designs at venues including Soho Theatre. *www.justindavid.co.uk*

Kino-Theatr opened in St Leonards in 1913 as a purpose-built cinema but got turned into a builders' merchant for many years before the current owners turned it back into a multi-purpose arts centre. *www.kino-teatr.co.uk*

Leaf Hall is an iconic building of historical interest, providing a space for the arts and entertainment for the people of Eastbourne. *www.leafhall.co.uk*

Latest Music Bar in Brighton is used for talks, spoken word, film screenings, club nights, art exhibitions, cabaret performances and fringe theatre, as well as their core music events. *www.latestmusicbar.co.uk*

Depot is an award-winning independent cinema in Lewes offering an innovative programme of mainstream and art house films along with special events and workshops. *www.lewesdepot.org*

Omnibus is a multi-award-winning independent theatre in Clapham, providing a platform for new writing and interdisciplinary work, and aiming to give voice to the underrepresented. *www.omnibus-clapham.org*

PRELUDE:

Valerie Solanas, *dressed in men's clothes and a cap, addresses the audience.*

Valerie Hey. Hi. I'm Valerie Solanas; founder of SCUM—the Society for Cutting Up Men. (*to a man in the audience*) It's ok, honey: you have nothing to fear—for now. (*beat*) OK. So we're going to start. Grab a drink, find a seat and please turn off your cell phones, cos nobody has them where we're going. New York. 1967. Let me set the scene: America is in the middle of the Summer of Love—and also the Vietnam war. At his studio, The Factory, Pop Artist Andy Warhol is making underground movies and instant Superstars. This year's Superstar is a foreign chick with only one name. I'd like you to meet my co-star...

A promo video introduces us to Nico, model, actress, singer with The Velvet Underground—and Andy Warhol 'Superstar'. All the while, the sound of an audience clapping, cheering has been growing as guitars are strummed and drumsticks count in.

As music begins, a spot snaps up on **Nico**, *wearing a pristine white suit. On the screen appears '1967', 'New York', 'Warhol's Exploding Plastic Inevitable'. She sings The Velvet Underground's Femme Fatale.*

Valerie's *speech is intercut with the song.*

Valerie (*to audience*) You can tell this song was written by a man. He doesn't get that she's not in to him. Men aren't too bright, on account of the male Y chromosome being an incomplete female X chromosome. They're walking abortions. Responsible, thrill-seeking females must overthrow the government...eliminate the money system...and destroy the male sex!

Music and lights snap off.

ONE:

Captions onscreen – '1967', 'New York', 'The Chelsea Hotel', 'Room 546'.

Lights snap up on darkened room in the Chelsea Hotel, traffic noise below. **Nico** *is passed out on the bed.* **Valerie** *stands at the door, holding a brown paper bag. She looks at* **Nico** *for a moment. Then, she makes her way towards her. Spots something on the floor. A tambourine. She picks it up and rattles it in* **Nico's** *ear.* **Nico** *wakes. Sees* **Valerie**. *Jumps.*

Valerie Hey. Hi.

Nico *stares at her.*

This is the Green Room, right? Has Warhol been in yet?

Nico *stares at her.*

You been waiting a while, huh?

Nico *stares at her.*

You look pretty relaxed.

Nico *stares at her.*

So...the fifth floor's where they keep the ritzy rooms. Velvet drapes!

Valerie *pokes her head around the curtains and a slither of solarised images appear on the screen. We can just make out images from early 60s ads featuring immaculate housewives, intercut with Nazi soldiers marching.*

How much did the *balcony* cost him? Hello down there! Jeez. I bet there's a *time delay!*

*The images disappear as **Valerie** pulls her head back again.*

I guess you're used to all this. It's great to be working with you! *(beat)* It is you, right? You're Nico?

*No response. **Valerie** waves a hand in front of **Nico**'s face.*

Hello? Is there anyone there?

Nico What...

Valerie Yes?

Pause.

Nico What is...?

Valerie What?

Pause.

Nico What is the...?

Valerie You can do it!

Nico What is the time?

Valerie *(checking her watch)* Nine a.m.

Nico Oh. What is the day?

Valerie *(beat)* Tuesday.

Nico Who are you?

Valerie Valerie Solanas!

Nico *stares at* **Valerie**.

Playwright. Performer. All around downtown legend. And the founder of 'SCUM': the Society for Cutting Up Men!

No recognition from **Nico**.

You wanna manifesto? *(produces SCUM Manifesto from her bag)* For men, two dollars. For women, one dollar. You want one?

Pause.

Nico No.

Pause.

Valerie So...Nico. It's an unusual name. Say; are you French?

Nico *searches for her boots.*

Where are you from?

Nico It is...not so interesting.

Valerie And what: you're the star of this thing?

Nico Err...

Valerie We're shooting a movie, right? *(no response)* Andy Warhol Productions? 'I, A Man'?

Nico Oh...yes. Is Jim here?

Valerie Jim who?

Nico Morrison. He is also in the movie.

Valerie For real?

Nico Jim is my love...

With a herculean effort, **Nico** *stands.*

Valerie Right! Do you have a script?

Nico There is no script. Andy likes just to watch what people do.

Valerie But that would be so boring!

Nico He says it is modern.

Valerie So you've been in one of his movies before?

Nico Yes. Chelsea Girls...

No recognition from **Valerie**.

The New York Times called it, 'A grotesque menagerie of lost souls whimpering in a psychedelic moonscape.'

Valerie Groovy.

Nico *goes to her case and begins rummaging through it. She pulls out garments and dumps them on* **Valerie**.

Valerie Woah. Those are some high-class threads.

Nico Hand-me-down rags, from who knows where...

Nico *finds her boots and with great concentration, pulls them on.*

Valerie *(picks up a handbag)* Dior! You must be making some serious dough!

Valerie *finds something in the bag and pockets it.*

Nico It was a gift from Brian Jones.

Valerie For real? What's he like?

Nico *makes a so-so gesture with her hand.*

Oh... You fucked? What was *that* like?

Nico I do not gossip with nobodies.

Valerie Well, aren't we the high-class ass! You gotta twat by Dior too?

Nico *snatches back the bag.*

You wanna watch out. I'm great at thinking on my feet. No script: no worries. Throw anything at me, I got a comeback. Hit me!

No response.

Any line you like!

Nico Was hast du genommen?

Valerie We get a scene together, I will fuck you up!

Nico We will not. Jim is in every scene, each time with a different girl.

Valerie Art imitates life... Wait: you know the plot?

Nico There is no plot.

Valerie You know *something*.

Nico Andy is not here yet.

Valerie Finally!

Nico If he was here, he would have come to see me.

Nico *retouches her make-up.* **Valerie** *picks up a scrapbook, opens it and reads.*

Valerie 'Nico: Mr Warhol's Silent Superstar!' *(beat)* See there's my problem: I like to talk. What's it like to be famous? What's it feel like to wake up in the morning and know you're going to be photographed and filmed and looked at all day long?

Nico Andy says that in the future, everybody will have fame for fifteen minutes.

Valerie Talking to Warhol is like talking to a chair. *(beat)* And he's cheap, you know? Twenty lousy bucks to be in a movie!

Nico Twenty dollars?

Valerie I never shoulda agreed to do it. But I need to talk to him about— *(realises something)* You're getting a lot more than twenty dollars, aren't you?

Nico So you think you can steal from me?

Valerie Hey. I'm no thief.

Nico Show me what you took from my bag.

Valerie *produces a Hershey bar.*

Valerie I'm hungry, OK?

Nico You are dieting?

Valerie No.

Nico Call room service.

Valerie Nobody from the hotel can know I'm here. *(beat)* I, er... lived here for a while. Room 303. Had a little trouble paying my rent.

Nico Everybody owes money to the Chelsea Hotel.

Valerie The manager held a knife to my neck, told me 'Never come back.'

Nico Stanley would not do that over rent.

Valerie He didn't like me entertaining gentlemen callers.

Nico In your room?

Valerie The elevator. *(beat)* I'm a writer. It was research. You see, I wrote a play—Up Your Ass. It's a great title, huh?

Nico It sounds dirty...

Valerie Thanks! *(the chocolate bar)* Can I eat this?

Nico *shrugs 'yes'.* **Valerie** *shoves it in to her mouth.*

So, it's about a man-hating prostitute, right? A mother strangles her son. A socialite gobbles a turd. I decided to give Warhol the opportunity to produce it. Did he show it to you?

Nico *(beat)* No.

Valerie Oh. But the two of you are tight?

Nico We are like Hansel and Gretel. Except I think he wants to be Gretel.

Valerie So you could talk my play up!

Nico Oh, you know...

Valerie You got to understand: it's a piece of me. It's like I literally gave him my firstborn.

Nico *throws herself on the bed with a groan.*

What's your deal? Why are you passed out alone in a darkened hotel room?

Nico Sunshine depresses me. There is too much expectation...

Valerie Like, staying conscious?

Nico Maybe you can help me.

Nico *digs in her handbag. Then her underwear...*

I need something to help my head.

Valerie An aspirin?

Nico I need to get straight.

Valerie Ah jeez...

Nico *(producing some cash)* I will give you twenty-six dollars...

Valerie That shit is the refuge of the mindless.

Nico I like that I can blow away my memory.

Valerie Stuff in your past, huh?

Beat.

Nico At The Factory, everybody dabbles. It is not a big deal...

Valerie You wanna be one of Warhol's whacked-out little robots?

Nico Andy calls me 'An IBM computer with a Garbo accent.'

Valerie You think that's funny?

Nico I have no sense of humour. I am German.

Valerie Oh: you're German!

Nico Not the kind who make lampshades of human skin. In fact, my family is really Russian... *(peeling off more notes)* Look: I will give you twenty-*eight* dollars.

Valerie Why'd you start on that shit anyway?

Nico All models take speed to stay slim.

Valerie Ad men like their women breakable. Sickos.

Nico Well, I am not. *(beat)* Brian Jones liked to slap me and punch me. And one time, when we were very high, he put a loaded gun in my...

Valerie In your pussy? Nice.

Nico But that night, the manager of the Stones took me to a public toilet and gave me the contract...

Valerie I guess blondes have more fun.

Nico It is more correct to say blondes have more money.

Valerie So that's why you came to America. Dollar!

Nico *(shrugs)* Andy heard my record. And he had a band that needed a singer.

Valerie The London Underground, right?

Nico Velvet Underground.

Valerie Don't tell me you slept with them too?

Nico Only John Cale. *(beat)* And Lou Reed.

Valerie Why'd you pass on the other two?

Nico I was tired.

Valerie Me, I'm also an entrepreneur—but I use my mouth.

Nico Oh yes?

Valerie Not like that! I sell conversation. Five cents a word. Two bucks for a short conversation. Four-fifty an hour. Men'll pay big to shoot the shit with a cunning linguist.

Nico Except when they do not, and you have to sell sex in the lift.

Valerie Hey. At least those transactions are honest. You got to pretend you like those music douchebags, and they gotta pretend to believe in your talent.

Nico Bitch.

Valerie Realist.

Nico *Jealous!*

Valerie Brian Jones give you that scar?

Nico Hmm?

Valerie On your belly. I noticed it when you were sleeping.

Nico *(beat)* No. I had a fight, with a Hell's Angel in a bar.

Valerie Sure you did.

Nico You think I could not fight you?

Valerie Nah.

Nico *(waving money at* **Valerie***)* Thirty dollars!

Valerie *(beat)* We're not talking about speed here, are we?

Nico Who pays thirty dollars for speed? You know what I want.

Valerie Look: this is The Chelsea. If you step outside, punks'll be queuing up to sell to you.

Nico Celebrities never score for themselves.

Valerie You don't need that shit!

Nico So you do not need my very good friend Andy?

Nico *indicates the phone. Beat.* **Valerie** *picks up the receiver and dials.*

Valerie *(on phone)* Hey, Sammi? It's Val. Listen: a friend needs a favour... No: not that... Not *that*!... Yeah. Chelsea Hotel: room 546: knock three times.

Valerie *replaces the receiver.* **Nico** *hands her some money.* **Valerie** *counts it.*

Nico It is nine, you say?

Valerie *(checks her watch)* Nine twenty.

Nico I do not like waiting for men.

Valerie The man's a woman. Butch dyke I used to room with.

Nico But we are like Hershey bars.

Valerie Excuse me?

Nico When I was a little girl in Berlin, there was no chocolate in the shops. We would beg the American soldiers for it, fight for it, prize it above all else. Then I come to New York, and there are rows and rows of Hershey bars, in every store, like they are nothing!

Valerie We are not nothing. You're a freaking Superstar! And I'm a great writer! But Warhol's sitting on the only copy of my play! It needs to be out there.

Nico Why?

Valerie Whaddya mean? It's three years of my life, and I can't write it again. Plus, it has this really important message, about how men—

Nico Maybe you should take drugs. You would think less.

Valerie I don't wanna think less! I want to think my thoughts and write them and have people hear what I've got to say!

Nico If you lose your shit, you lose all of your power.

Valerie I don't wanna be some silent sex doll, OK?

Beat.

Nico I think I will call Stanley...

Valerie Oh—listen—I didn't mean to offend you!

Nico Go.

Valerie If you kick me out, you're not gonna get your fix.

Beat.

Nico Blackmail? I thought you were on the side of women?

Valerie Only the ones who are fit to join SCUM.

Nico The Society for Cutting Up Men...

Valerie Damn straight.

Nico If you had a society for cutting up Jews, do you think you would be tolerated in New York?

Valerie Look; surely you can see that men get all the best gigs in this town? In life! But that's not cause they're better than women. The only thing that someone like Warhol is better at is public relations. *Telling* everyone how great he is. SCUM can change that.

Nico Hmm. How many members do you have?

Valerie Well, you see—SCUM is less of an organisation and more of a *state of mind*...

Nico How many?

Valerie So far? Just me.

Nico Ho, ho, ho.

Valerie I'm looking to recruit...

Nico I do not like marching. Marching is for soldiers, singing 'Deutschland Uber Alles'.

Valerie So you're happy to cling to Daddy.

Nico I never even knew my father...

Valerie What's Warhol? What's Jim, if not a Daddy substitute?

Nico He is the first man I have met who is not afraid of me in some way.

Valerie Yeah? Well, men should be afraid. 'Cause when SCUM strikes, it'll be in the dark with a six inch blade.

Nico *(contemptuous)* Oh, really!

Valerie And if we ever march, it'll be over the President's stupid, sickening face.

Nico *starts to sing 'Das Lied Der Deutschen'—quietly at first, rising in volume.*

Nico *(sings)* Von der mass bis an die memel

Valerie SCUM will fuck up the system, destroy property, murder—annihilate every last lowly turd in the world—

Nico *(sings)* Von der etsch bis an den belt

Valerie Squash, step on, crush and crunch every man! And the sensible ones, they won't make a distressing fuss—

Nico *(sings)* DEUTSCHLAND DEUTSCHLAND UBER ALLES

Valerie They'll just ride the waves to their demise.

Nico UBER ALLES IN DER WELT

A knock at the door.

Nico Thank God!

Valerie Wait: that's not the code.

Nico It must be my call. Tell them I need more time. I need to be perfect for Jim.

Valerie *(deadpan)* You have a pussy and a pulse.

Nico I cannot go out there until the man...woman has come!

Valerie *(beat)* You better *rave* about my play.

Nico *nods.* **Valerie** *exits.* **Nico** *compulsively piles on powder.* **Valerie** *returns, terrified.*

Nico What is the matter? Is it the manager?

Frozen to the spot, **Valerie** *shakes her head.*

The police?

Valerie It's *my* call!

Nico There has been some mistake. They should want me first.

Valerie He asked for Miss Solanas. *(beat)* Jeez: what am I going to do?

Nico Act?

Valerie I'm playing myself.

Nico Bad luck.

Valerie I really need Warhol to like me. Would it kill you to help me?!

Nico *(beat)* Just let Jim seduce you.

Valerie That's maybe what you'd do.

Nico Fine. Do what you want.

Valerie *(having an idea)* Yeah. I will.

Valerie *grabs her brown paper bag and goes to the door.*

Nico What if the woman comes?

Valerie She won't.

Nico What?!

Valerie Not yet, anyways. *(pulls a Manifesto from her bag)* While I'm gone, I'll let you take a peek at my Manifesto. *(hands **Nico** the Manifesto)* For free!

Nico *(hands back the manifesto)* I do not like to read.

Valerie You're right: SCUM's not for you. It's for whores, dykes, criminals and homicidal maniacs! See you later, Daddy's Girl.

Nico Tell me. The men get cut up... What do the women get?

Valerie *(thinks, is stumped)* Fired, if they don't get their asses on set.

Valerie *exits.*

INTERLUDE 1:

A spot snaps up on **Valerie**, *with the manifesto still in her hand. (The following may be part improvised in the manner of a stand-up as she interacts with the audience.)*

Valerie Me again. Did you miss me? You did, didn't you? *(to a woman)* I can tell *you* did...

She addresses a man in the audience.

Hey. Hey you. What's your name? *(listens to the response)* Gimme a dollar, 'Jeff', and I'll give you a dirty word. You don't got a dollar? Gimme a beer. Two beers. *(points to pre-set bottles of beer, coaxes 'Jeff' to hand them to her)* Thanks. Here's your dirty word: are you ready? 'Men'. To call a man an animal is to flatter him. Watch this. Hey. 'Jeff'. You're an animal! See? He's flattered! Of course he is! He'd like to be big and strong and fierce and horny. Wouldn't you, tiger? *(beat)* You're a machine. A dildo with legs. You'd swim through a river of snot, wade nostril-deep through a mile of vomit, if you thought there was a friendly pussy waiting for you at the end of it. Ladies: you know what I'm talking about. *(she picks a woman in the audience)* Hey sweetheart? What's your name? *(listens for the response)* 'Lucy', you know what I'm talking about, right? But, listen, I'm done with talking about the men. 'Jeff', he's had his moment in the spotlight. All you men have. Now it's time—finally—for us badass women to get ours. Am I right? 'Lucy', am I right?' 'Lucy', do you want to join SCUM? You won't literally have to cut up any men. Unless you want to. *(keeps going until 'Lucy' says yes)* Great! Now listen: if I asked you to drop everything tomorrow and devote your life to female revolution, *could* you? *(assuming she says no)* Why not? *(assuming she says she has to work)* What's your job? *(let's assume she does HR for Google)* See: 'Lucy' can't join the female revolution cos she's spending her waking hours trying to make rent cos she's earning twenty percent less, fending off her creepy manager and probably doing most of the housework—but I digress. Ladies: listen up: I have a revolutionary plan. We're going to refuse to work. I don't mean 'drop out': smoking hash in your underwear never changed shit. No: SCUM will *un*work. It'll go like this: saleswomen won't charge for merchandise; factory workers will secretly destroy equipment. 'Lucy' here is going to go in to Google HQ and delete all the HR files so nobody will know who's meant to be working there anyway. 'Lucy': are you down with that? *(waits for a response)* SCUM will unwork at a job until we get fired, then get a new job to unwork at and so on—until we bring the economy to its knees! Oh, and we're going to stop buying things. We're just going to loot. We're gonna loot, fuck up and kill—if we have to— until we destroy the money-work system! In a moneyless society, nobody has power over anyone else. All non-creative jobs will be done by machines—whilst we build Utopia. Who's in? I said 'who's in'? *(waits for audience response)* Alright: stand by for further instructions...

She picks up the beers and bag.

I've been Valerie Solanas, and you've all been—SCUM.

Lights snap off.

TWO:

Onscreen title: 1967. Snap up on The Chelsea Hotel. **Nico**, *alone, in a high state of agitation.*

Nico Shit! Shit: that bitch!

Valerie *enters, carrying two beer bottles and her bag.* **Nico** *immediately assumes the mask of 'Superstar' again.*

Valerie Ask me how my scene went down.

Nico You came back.

Valerie I totally schooled my co-star! Warhol loved it. Well, I figure he loved it. By the time they called 'cut' he was gone.

Nico I thought you had gone.

Valerie I had to come back. I didn't get a chance to speak to Warhol yet.

Nico Forever.

Valerie You thought I'd take your money and run? I'm not an asshole. Hey: I got something for you!

Nico *(suddenly animated)* Oh yes?

Valerie I cadged some beer off the crew...

Huge disappointment from **Nico**.

It's German!

Nico I hate Germans.

Valerie Yeah: I hate Minnesotans. *(swigs her beer)* I ask Tom: do you dig men? He says, yeah: as friends.

Nico Who is Tom?

Valerie Dude in my scene.

Nico But the only man in the film is Jim...

Nico *starts to repair her make-up.*

Valerie I ask, you dig them romantically? Sexually? He says his instincts tell him to dig chicks. I say, so do mine. Why should my status be lower than yours? *(beat)* Jeez—if you add another layer, you'll be in drag.

Nico This—this make up—is Nico.

Valerie You think you're just your make-up?

Nico No: I invented the character of a girl singer and named her Nico.

Valerie Yeah? What's your real name?

Nico It is not so interesting.

Valerie Ah Christ—not you too! All the Stupidstars at Warhol's Factory, they're always trying to be something else. Heiresses wanna be junkies. Boys wanna be girls...

Nico You dress like a boy.

Valerie I dress like a dyke.

Nico We are both in drag. If this was Berlin, we could be an act in the cabaret.

Valerie *grabs a hat from* **Nico**'s *case. Puts it on. Poses.*

Valerie *(cod German)* Ladies unt Gentlemen—

Nico *grabs the hat.*

Valerie Meanie!

Valerie *grabs for the hat:* **Nico** *whips it away and sticks it on her own head. She turns away.* **Valerie** *makes a gun with two fingers. Points it at* **Nico**.

Valerie Hey. Look at me.

Nico *turns to face* **Valerie**.

Hand it over.

Beat. **Valerie** *uses her 'finger gun' to tip the hat off* **Nico**'s *head.*

Nico Sei nicht kindisch!

Valerie *examines herself in the mirror.*

Valerie I like it. Can I have it?

Nico It belongs to Jim.

Valerie It's a genuine Lizard King artefact? Groovy! *(as Jim)* I'm Jim Morrison. My status is higher than yours: I'm gonna make you wait. But when *I* want it, you better leap to attention! *(as Jim)* C'mon baby, light my fire... C'mon baby, light my fiirrree!

Valerie *goes in to enthusiastic air guitar. The 'guitar' becomes a cock. She* *ends by grabbing* **Nico** *and bumping and grinding against her leg.* **Nico** *grabs her.*

Whaaa?!

Nico The woman is definitely coming?

Valerie Sure.

Nico You would not just say she was coming?

Valerie A beer'll take the edge off *(she holds out a beer)* C'mon.

Nico I...do not drink Paffgen's beer.

Valerie Why not?

Nico It is shit.

Valerie I got it for you special! OK: it ain't French champagne, but you take a few sips, to be friendly.

Nico We are not friends.

Valerie No! You know why? We have nothing in common. Nobody handed me anything: I had to fight.

Nico You think I do not?

Valerie Naked?

Nico I am hustling, each time I meet Andy or Lou or Bob Dylan.

Valerie Good Old Nico! Still being nice to Americans for candy.

Nico I am a professional. I keep my real life private. Like Garbo.

Valerie That dame has all the hallmarks of a depressive egomaniac.

Nico You know psychology?

Valerie I gotta PHD.

Nico What happened?

Valerie Nobody wanted to employ a lady scientist. But hey: I got my conversational gig. Flexible hours. Independence. Excellent opportunities for travel—around and around the block.

Nico You are homeless?

Valerie I reside on a rooftop! With sweeping vistas of Manhattan!

Nico That is not really glamorous...

Valerie *(beat)* Look: I'll level with you. Yeah: the roof sucks. Sucks the big one. If it's cold, I wear all my clothes and I still freeze. Sometimes, I'm so hungry, I eat pieces of grocery bag. And it's tempting: my god is it tempting! to just slip under. Some nights, I'd like to lie down and never wake up.

Nico *(beat)* After the war, the Russians stopped all supplies to West Berlin. I was always cold and hungry.

Valerie Then you know where I'm coming from. *(beat)* Aren't your family Russian?

Nico No, Turkish. It is gauche to talk about hardship. It makes people uncomfortable.

Valerie But I got the answer to all of society's problems right here! *(her Manifesto)* And when it gets published, and Andy produces my play, I'll have the world by the balls! Someday, this bottle *(her beer)* will be worth more than that hat.

Nico You think you are going to be bigger than Jim Morrison?

Valerie Hey. If the hat fits...

Nico The world does not want a female Jim Morrison.

Valerie Tough!

Nico Of course, you are going to change its mind, single-handed!

Valerie With the Sisterhood.

Nico It is curious... You have not treated me as a sister. Only as a stepping stone to Andy.

Valerie *(beat)* That's not true.

Nico You have done nothing but insult me—yet you do not even know me.

Valerie OK: tell me about you. What was it like growing up in a war zone? *(beat)* Must've been pretty scary?

Nico The past is unimportant.

Valerie It's how we know who we are.

Nico In the forests and palaces of the imagination, time is meaningless...

Valerie If you want to change your future, you gotta stop doing the same old shit.

Nico Like constantly bugging Andy?

Valerie Right now, I'm famous for fifteen people. Fourteen of those are drag queens!

Nico Why do you want a man to produce your play?

Valerie I tried every female producer in New York. Both of them. They said it was too angry. Too dirty. Warhol's movies are the dirtiest thing in Manhattan: I thought for sure he'd be down with Up Your Ass.

Nico Perhaps your message isn't the problem—but your delivery.

Valerie *(beat)* Did he say something?

Nico Everyone prefers greetings cards to letter bombs. You know, you have beautiful lips.

Valerie Are you coming on to me?

Nico They *could* look very good on the camera. All it would take is a little... Do you have make-up in that bag of yours?

Valerie Ha! *(beat)* No.

Nico *produces a lipstick. Uncaps it. Advances towards* **Valerie**, *who shies away.*

Nico What is the matter? Are you scared?

Valerie No woman could be scared of something that size.

Nico A little glamour might get Andy back on your side.

Valerie So you think he's pissed with me?

Nico Make the pout.

Valerie *makes a sulky pout.* **Nico** *applies lipstick to her lips.*

You know 'glamour' is a spell? Subtle as smoke, it can slide into people's souls… And before they even know it—they want you. They cannot live without you! And you gave away nothing.

Nico *shows* **Valerie** *her reflection.*

Valerie I look like a trucker in drag.

Nico You think you are smart. You are being self-destructive.

Valerie I'm being me.

Nico Never, ever give them that.

Nico *grabs a scarf.*

Essaye-ca!

Nico *puts it on* **Valerie** *and styles her.*

Ah! Tu es si belle, ma cherie! And now you will seduce me.

Valerie With pleasure!

Nico Pretend I am Andy.

Valerie Oh. OK.

Nico So.

Nico *takes up some semblance of a Warhol stance.*

Valerie Nah; the hand's faggier...

Nico *changes her hand position.*

Too much: that's Liberace...

Nico *changes again.*

Alright.

Nico *(as Warhol)* Oh hey, Valerie.

Valerie *(clapping* **Nico** *on the back)* Andy, you cocksucker. When are you going to do my play?

Nico *(as Warhol)* Taxi!

Valerie What?

Nico *(as herself)* Act grateful!

Nico *assumes the Warhol stance again.*

Valerie Say, Andy: I was, um, I was really proud when you asked me to be in your movie.

Nico *(as Warhol)* Oh? You were?

Valerie You can see I got something—something new and fresh that—

Nico *(as Warhol)* Gee: I guess it's all about you... *(as herself)* Talk about him!

Valerie I really admire you. I'd love to hear more. Could I maybe buy you a coffee?

Nico Wunderschone! Now ask him where Jim is.

Valerie This again?

Nico Perhaps he has phoned him.

Valerie Here's a crazy idea. Stop wasting your energy on people who don't respect you.

Nico Fine.

Nico *turns her back on* **Valerie.**

Valerie When did I not respect you?

Nico 'A silent sex doll'?

Valerie Oh God. About that—

Nico I speak four languages.

Valerie I'd be the last person to judge somebody for who they sleep with.

Nico I have been a success in three different industries. And I can cook cauliflower cheese.

Valerie There's a lot more to you than meets the eye. But you dance to their tune.

Nico It is their party.

Three knocks at the door.

My delivery?

Valerie *nods.*

Thank God!

Nico *goes for the door.* **Valerie** *halts her.*

Valerie Allow me.

Valerie *painstakingly walks to the door.*

Nico Hurry!

Valerie I am answering the door like a *lady*.

Valerie *glides into the darkness of the corridor. Re-enters, with a small package.*

Nico Give it to me.

Valerie *whips it away*

I paid for it!

Valerie What: you're gonna call the cops?

Nico *tries to grab the drugs.* **Valerie** *puts them in her top pocket.*

Nico You can have the hat.

Valerie No.

Nico My clothes, the rest of my money.

Valerie Just tell me what they do for you. Why are they so fucking great?

Nico They make my good thoughts run slower and my bad thoughts go away.

Valerie What else?

Nico They turn day into night.

Valerie What else?

Nico They are like a seduction.

Valerie By death.

Nico I would take death over Lou Reed any day.

Valerie Ah.

Nico Since we split up, he wants to take all my songs from me.

Valerie Well, listen: what you put up with is what you get. *(picking up a pair of dark glasses)* So. I'll play Lou Reed.

Nico But...how will this help me?

Valerie The drugs are not your problem. And if you figure out your problem, you won't need the drugs. So: I'm Lou Reed. *(she puts on the glasses. Then, as Lou)* Hey, Nico.

Nico He is not so friendly...

Valerie *(as Lou)* Hey, Bitch!

Nico *tries to hit* **Valerie**.

Valerie Woah, woah, woah!

Nico Lou is...formal to me now.

Valerie OK. *(as Lou)* Good morning, Nico.

Nico Lou... You know in the band, I only have three songs to sing?

Valerie *(as Lou)* Because I wrote them.

Nico But what should I do on stage when I am not singing?

Valerie *(as Lou)* Well, Nico—you can always knit. *(then as herself)* Go on!

Nico I do not want to knit.

Valerie Good!

Nico And I also do not want to play the fucking tambourine. It is not a real instrument!

Valerie *(as Lou)* So stay off the stage.

Nico Go to hell!

Valerie Attagirl!

Nico I have seen hell, I have smelt it. Berlin was a wilderness of bricks. Bodies in the rubble. A graveyard at the end of our street that I would play in.

Valerie I think you like misery, huh?

Nico I *like* it?

Valerie Well: what are you doing? Hanging around with those creeps, who just barely let you rattle a tambourine?

Nico I am a star.

Valerie Yeah: famous for being *silent!*

Nico 'Miss Pop 1966'.

Valerie It's 1967. So what you gonna do now?

Nico Drugs.

Valerie *shakes the tambourine in her face.*

I cannot just leave the band.

Valerie *shakes the tambourine in her face.* **Nico** *grabs it.*

I made a solo album. Chelsea Girls, like the film.

Valerie OK...

Nico See—you have not heard of it! That is because it was sabotaged by the producer!

Valerie How?

Nico He brought in a flute player! Forced that flute in to every inch of my record. When I heard it, I cried! *(beat)* Are you laughing at me?

Valerie *(yes)* No! The guy...violated your art.

Nico You *are* laughing!

Valerie No I'm not!

Valerie *bursts out laughing.* **Nico** *joins in. And then* **Nico** *is crying.*

Nico It was shit. It was shit. It was just so shit...

Valerie The thing with letting other people solve your problems: you have to live with their shitty solutions.

Nico I did not give up. I wrote new songs and asked John Cale to produce them. He said, 'Nico: how do you sell suicide?'

Valerie Rude!

Nico But Jim said, 'Christa: you should make your own music.' So I got a harmonium.

Valerie Christa? That your real name? *(No response)* It's pretty. Why'd you change it?

Nico Coco Chanel named me Nico, after we had an affair.

Valerie For real?

Nico Or my gay best friend called me after a boy he liked.

Valerie Which one's true?

Nico The press take down everything I say: it is so silly!

Valerie You're just a little tease? I guess Lou Reed was right.

Beat.

Nico I was christened on Kristellnacht, when they smashed up the shops of the Jews. The broken glass sparkled on the sidewalk as my father walked out on my mother and me. And then he got shot by the Nazis.

Valerie Shit. I'm sorry.

Nico Why? He was also a Nazi. He gave me only my tallness, and a name. Christa Päffgen.

Valerie Päffgen? Like the beer? Is that your family?

Nico No. When I found them, as a teenager, my father's family were clear. His bastard was not to have one penny from their brewery. Or come near them again.

Valerie Tch! Sex is the root of all evil.

Nico I like to have sex. Don't you?

Valerie Sex with me... I mean, I can't be bothered. I've seen the whole scene, anyways.

Nico You have tried everything?

Valerie My stepfather took me when I was ten. So, you know, I started early.

Nico No wonder you are a lesbian...

Valerie No wonder you cling to Daddy substitutes!

Nico Jim...makes me happy.

Valerie Your idea of happiness is a graveyard. A graveyard that's been bombed.

Nico Love is a joke to you.

Valerie No. At fourteen, at boarding school, I loved a girl with the whole of my soul.

Nico Tell me about her. Was she pretty?

Valerie Real pretty. But when they caught us together, they kicked her out.

Nico Bad girls always get banished. Like in the fairytale.

Valerie There's a fairytale for dykes?

Nico Once there was a girl who was on fire. And the flames raged inside her and she was in agony. But nobody in the village would help, for fear she would burn down their homes. They banished her to the desert, to wander forever. And she was so hungry but everything tasted of ashes and she was so lonely but her tears turned to steam on her cheeks. Then one day, a tall girl with yellow hair appeared, dressed in a velvet cloak that was blacker than night. She said, let me wrap it around you, to douse the flames. The girl was afraid. The cloak was so big and so black that she thought she might disappear. But our heroine said, don't be scared. We will do it together.

Valerie So what happens?

Nico They do the smack together.

Valerie Aw, c'mon...

Nico The first time is better than any orgasm ever.

Valerie For real?

Nico Let me show you a happy ending...

Nico *leans in for a kiss. But at the last moment,* **Valerie** *pulls away.*

Valerie This isn't a fucking fairytale. You're lousy with movie roles and money and fame! Everything I ever wanted! And if you don't grab your fifteen minutes and make them work for you, you're a putz.

Nico I am not some one hit wonder.

Valerie You might get a year. That's about the shelf life of a Warhol Superstar.

Nico What would you know?

Valerie That skinny heiress who was all over the papers with him last year—

Nico Edie.

Valerie What happened to her?

Nico She was a junkie.

Valerie *waves the drugs in front of her—then whisks them away.*

Valerie Look: what's the worst that could happen? You fail.

Nico And then I do not have money. And it is not just me.

Valerie *(beat)* Oh. That scar on your belly. It's from a Caesarean.

Nico A scimitar in an opium den!

Valerie How old's your kid?

Nico *(beat)* Ari is six.

Valerie Is Jim...?

Nico No: his father is French. I need air.

Nico *draws the curtains completely and solarised images fill the screen: Nazi soldiers and sixties idealised American mothers.* **Nico** *goes on to the balcony.*

Valerie Nico?

Silence. **Valerie** *joins* **Nico** *on the balcony.*

Christa?

Nico *is staring over the edge.*

Nico Jim and I stayed in a castle. Of course, there are no real castles in California—but it had battlements. One night, very drunk, he walked naked around the edge, and he dared me to follow.

Valerie Did you?

Nico It was spoilt rock star bullshit. No.

Valerie Good for you.

Nico It was not creative: it was not destructive. It changed nothing.

Valerie The male rebel is a farce. They invented the goddam rules! *(beat)* So you do want change?

Nico If I change my *hairstyle*, I am risking my whole career!

Valerie What if you moved back to Germany?

Nico Do you know what I had to do to get out of that war-torn shithole? *(beat)* I wish I had been born a man.

Valerie That's like wishing to be born retarded.

Valerie *joins* **Nico** *at the rail. Pause.*

Look at them, down there. Regular Josephines with their regular Josephine lives. Wondering if they can really pull off that mini skirt. If their husband knows they fake it. Whether they bought enough beer to keep him sweet... The crazy thing is: if all women left their men, unworked their jobs and banded together...we could create a magic world!

Nico *(re: the drugs)* I have a magic world.

Valerie Contemplating your navel isn't the answer!

Nico What would the Josephines do, if a person dropped from the sky?

Beat.

Valerie If you jump and you land on your feet, your thigh bones puncture your guts.

Nico What do you think happens after? Me, I am superstitious. I believe in heaven and hell.

Valerie And where d'you think you'd end up?

Nico Berlin. *(Beat.)* The ruins are in all my dreams. They are where I go in my mind on the subway and sometimes in bed.

Valerie You remind me of a friend. He'd been in Vietnam. Woke up every morning screaming.

Nico What happened to him?

Valerie Left a note, said he'd gone somewhere quiet.

Nico The drugs make my head quiet.

Nico *reaches for the drugs.* **Valerie** *whips them away.*

Fine.

Nico *steps towards the edge of the balcony.*

Valerie Don't you dare pull that Jim Morrison bullshit.

Nico I am not

Beat.

Valerie You have a kid.

Nico He will forget me.

Valerie Kids never forget their mothers.

Nico They never forgive them.

Valerie Where is he?

Nico Last night, his grandmother came and took him to Spain.

Valerie For a vacation?

Nico I sing in nightclubs. I do not trust the sitters, so I take him with me. And then he stays up all night. Drinks the dregs from people's glasses. The doctor said he has jaundice. She is right; he is better without me.

Nico *steps towards the edge of the balcony.* **Valerie** *grabs her arm. Pulls her back to safety.*

Valerie Let me tell you something. That boarding school I went to? It was a home for wayward girls.

Nico Wayward?

Valerie Knocked up.

Nico You had a baby?

Valerie A son. And a daughter. I gave them up for adoption.

Nico Both children!

Valerie The hand that rocks the cradle can't rock the boat.

Nico Tch!

Valerie Look: this way, our kids get great lives—and we get to be who we want! Hey: you wanna write songs for my play? It's about this trick-turning, wise-cracking, totally misanthropic dyke!

Nico I want to be Ari's mother.

Valerie *(beat)* I stopped visiting David and Linda cause it hurt too much to leave. You gotta go all in.

Nico If I marry Jim, I can get him back.

Valerie Once SCUM destroys the money system, you won't

have to fuck for childcare.

Nico Jim is my soulmate. We cut our thumbs with a knife and let our blood mingle.

Valerie OK.

Nico I have worked from the age of fourteen! And my son is my life. It is bullshit, to say we must choose! How is that radical?

Valerie I'm not saying I like it...

Nico We will be a family. And Jim will help me make songs.

Valerie You think he'll, what? Babysit whilst you write?

Nico Why not?

Valerie *Jim Morrison?!*

Nico Why are my words less important?

Valerie *(beat)* They're not. You're not going to tiptoe round the edge of his castle.

Nico I will burn the place down.

Valerie You can do what you want. But not with a big, fat wrap in your hand.

Nico *(looks at **Valerie**, beat)* OK. Throw the stuff away.

Valerie No. *(beat)* You're gonna do it.

Valerie *gives the drugs to* **Nico**. *A hesitation. Then she finally throws them over the balcony and steps away from the edge. (*She pretends to throw* *them away, but hides them in her hand).*

Good for—

Nico I am sick.

Nico *goes back in to the room.* **Valerie** *follows.*

Valerie Christa?

Nico Sick of waiting!

Nico *exits.*

Valerie *goes to the case (looking for more food). Finds a script. Looks at the cover page. Opens it and starts to read. Lights snap off.*

INTERLUDE 2:

A spot snaps up on **Nico** *at the harmonium. Onscreen: '1974', 'The Roundhouse, London' appear in a white seventies gothic typeface.*

Nico My manager says I should talk to the audience. And smile. It will make me seem…friendly. *(she flicks on a dead smile, flicks it off again)* You know, when I was a model, almost two thousand years ago, they were always telling us to be 'friendly' to the photographers, the buyers, the creepy old clients… *(beat)* But now… I'm an artist, not a mannequin. If you wanted somebody friendly, you shouldn't have come to see me.

Nico *plays the harmonium, awkwardly then gaining confidence. Images of key feminist moments from 1967-86 emerge from the darkness as she sings her own song 'Afraid'.*

As she stops playing, the images stop emerging and the light snaps off.

THREE:

Caption onscreen: 1967. Lights snap up on The Chelsea Hotel. **Valerie** *is reading the script.*

Valerie Shit. That bastard.

She drops the script.

The bastard!

Collapses on the bed. **Nico** *enters.*

Nico They have gone!

Valerie What?

Nico All of them! And the equipment.

Nico *kicks the suitcase.*

Valerie Hey. We expect it, right? Men are flakey. Oversensitive. Say one wrong thing, and they just flounce off!

Nico *(beat)* What did you do?

Valerie Me?

Nico You said something to Andy.

Valerie *(sitting up)* Why don't you sit down, fix your hair?

Nico Tell me.

Valerie I could give you a little shoulder massage?

Nico Just tell me what you said to Andy!

Valerie I might've kinda threatened to staple his wig to his balls.

Nico My God.

Valerie I was joking!

Nico Shit! What am I going to tell Jim? When he comes, and there is no filming, he will think I have fooled him.

Valerie Get real, lady! Jim's not coming.

Nico Yes. He is just being...held off.

Valerie *Sucked* off.

Nico We will be married.

Valerie Jim Morrison is not gonna marry you. He's the star most likely to hump himself to death!

Nico You do not know—

Valerie Oh, I do know! We're both getting totally screwed here! And you know what the lesson is? We can only rely on ourselves. *(beat)* We'll call the press. Expose Warhol for what he is: an exploiter of women!

Nico Do what you want.

Valerie No-one will listen to me. But you're famous. You have a responsibility!

Nico *grabs her suitcase, starts throwing things in to it.*

But—what? You're just going to give up and go home? *(beat)* No: you're running off to the next sadistic bastard. Who'll treat you like the piece of shit you think you are.

Nico My God. All you do is to *talk*. About what is wrong with men, how they've fucked up the world. Writing your little plays, your little pamphlets—

Valerie It's a Manifesto!

Nico I do not want to hear it! Because, you think you are solving anything, by ranting all the time?

Valerie If you don't speak out, you're colluding in their shitty system!

Nico *shuts the case and goes to leave.* **Valerie** *blocks her path.*

Nico Get out of my way!

Valerie I'm trying to free you! I'm the *good* guy here!

Nico Yes! Americans always think they are the good guys.

Valerie Look—Christa—

Nico Halt deinem mund!

Beat. **Valerie** *steps out of* **Nico***'s way.* **Nico** *goes towards the door—but as she does, her suitcase comes open. Clothes fall out on to the floor. Pause.*

In Berlin, the GIs strutted around like we owed them. I heard the whispers of women in powder rooms and changing cubicles and hair salons. 'Avoid Tauentzienstrasse after 6pm.' 'Never linger: keep moving.' 'Having your child with you will not stop them.' At the age of fourteen, I did not understand—but everywhere that I went, I could feel their eyes.

Valerie Perverts love a schoolgirl...

Nico I had a job. As an office girl at the American base. One night, I'm kept late. It's just me and one Sergeant. I focus on the papers I am supposed to be filing—but from across the office, I can feel him staring. 'Komm, frau.' A whisper in bad German. He knows my name but does not use it. I go to him. He shuts the door. Pulls me close. And kisses me like Gene Kelly in the movies! Then throws me against the door and pushes up my skirt. Afterwards, I stay there, pressed into that doorway, for a long time. Then I pull down my skirt and say, may I go home? Back in our empty apartment—my mother is out with a boyfriend—I drink half a bottle of schnapps and get in the bath—and all that I feel is relief. Because it has happened. No more waiting.

Valerie *(beat)* I woulda cut his fucking balls off.

Nico You would have taken the carton of cigarettes and kept your mouth shut. That is war.

Valerie And what Brian Jones did to you wasn't?

Pause.

Nico Boys pretend to be soldiers. Some of them never grow out of it.

Valerie Because nobody makes them!

Nico Well, I could not shut my mouth. When my mother came home next morning, I told her what that Sergeant had done. She went to his CO. And then other girls came forward and the man was court martialled. I had to testify. They shot him.

Valerie Good!

Nico I do not know if they shot him for what he did, or because he was black.

Beat.

Valerie He was a rapist.

Nico I killed him.

Valerie You were a kid. *(beat)* I was fourteen when I had my first child. Too many girls have the same story.

Nico *(making for the door)* Those women were right: shut up and keep moving.

Valerie No. We're going to stand firm. Call them out. Can't you feel it, out there? The rage of generations of women—reaching boiling point! You're not alone. *We're* not. We'll lead a revolution!

Nico I do not want to kill any more men.

Valerie It's not women versus men! It's SCUM versus everyone else. We'll build a new society—where *nobody* gets exploited.

Nico I am fine.

Valerie You don't have to play the tough girl with me.

Valerie *goes to* **Nico.** *Beat. She puts her arm around her.* **Nico** *doesn't resist.*

You suck at it, anyway.

Nico Bitch

Valerie Realist.

Nico You think you are such a bad ass…

Valerie Hey. I'm not gonna let anyone hurt you, ever again.

Nico What do you mean?

Valerie I know—you know—that the meaning of life is love. Not dependency or sex, but friendship; friendship based upon respect. Love can only exist between two secure, free-wheeling, independent, groovy females.

Valerie *tries to kiss* **Nico**. **Nico** *pulls away, then smacks her round the face.* **Valerie** *bursts in to tears.*

I showed you my soul, and you're throwing it back in my face?

Nico Hit me back.

Valerie No.

Nico *shoves* **Valerie**.

Nico Hard.

Valerie You better be damn sure: I'm a pro.

Nico You think I lied about that Hell's Angel? I did not, though I lie about everything else. *(produces the wrap from her pocket)* Look. I am a total phoney!

Valerie *knocks the wrap from* **Nico's** *hand.*

Valerie You don't need that shit—you need me.

Nico You stupid bitch.

Nico *grabs* **Valerie.** *They wrestle.*

You have been asking for it all day!

Nico *pins* **Valerie** *down on the floor.*

I am going to teach you a fucking lesson!

Valerie Do what you want! I'm not going to give up on you.

Beat. **Nico** *lets* **Valerie** *go.*

Nico I...am not in love with you.

Valerie Cos I don't got a dick?

Nico I have loved women. And hated some of them.

Valerie Do you hate me?

Nico It is the same with men. I have to believe that some of them really are good guys.

Valerie Like Warhol?

Nico Andy is my friend.

Valerie Do you hate me?

Nico (beat) No.

Nico *pockets the wrap.*

Valerie Then please. Be honest. Has he mentioned my play?

Nico Uhh...

Valerie He show it to you?

Nico So many scripts: it is hard to remember...

Valerie The truth, Christa.

Nico *(beat)* Some of us read it aloud.

Valerie For Andy? What did he think?

Nico It made him laugh.

Valerie I knew it!

Nico But it was so dirty, he said it must be entrapment. He thought you were a lady cop!

Valerie For real?!

Nico Well, you would not stop calling.

Valerie I needed to talk to him! And he was always out! *(beat)* He wasn't out, was he?

Nico I will be straight: he has been avoiding you. He lost your play.

Valerie Lost it?

Nico He was in Max's with Candy and Viva and Mick Jagger and it...disappeared.

Valerie He didn't lose it. *(grabbing the screenplay)* Is this his next movie?

Nico Uh...?

Valerie This one has a script. 'Women In Revolt. By Andy Warhol and Paul Morrissey.' But listen, *(opens the script and reads)* 'You know that men are inferior to females, right?' and then 'Men have been conning women since time began that woman is no good...' Those lines are mine. Tons of the lines are mine. This is assault!

Nico I do not—

Valerie Big man with his big dick tearing off a big piece!

Valerie *rips up the script of Women In Revolt.*

That son of a bitch. Twenty bucks. He thought he could buy me off with twenty lousy bucks...

Nico *rummages in her case.*

Nico *(produces some tin foil)* Look: I could talk to him... *(produces a bent and blackened spoon)* Ask him to pay you properly... *(produces a candle)* In fact, I will go to him now!

Valerie That's a nice offer.

Nico *(rummaging in her case)* Have you seen a lemon?

Valerie I appreciate it.

Nico The lemon is not in my suitcase...

Valerie But don't bother...

Nico Perhaps it has rolled somewhere...

Valerie There's no lemon, and no point.

Nico *looks behind the bed.*

Is that where he's hidden the cameras?

Nico *(beat)* What cameras?

Valerie Warhol likes to watch people. Sure. He has no ideas of his own. Campbell's soup cans. Brillo boxes. Everything he ever does is a knock off! He'll steal my Manifesto. All my new stuff! Everything!

From here, the lighting slowly dims. On screen, we see images of marching Nazis, 60s alcohol ads that verge on soft porn. They degrade as the scene progresses.

They fear me—because I'm a scientist. Yeah—that's it.

Nico They?

Valerie I know that the male Y gene is an incomplete female X. And they know that I know that! All the rich, white men: they're terrified! SCUM could blow the whole show!

Nico What do you mean?

Valerie Up to now, they've grabbed whatever they wanted. The money, the oil, the power, the glory! My career. My girlfriend. My childhood. My children. *(very upset)* You know: I'd love to drop out. Be numb—but I can't. We're more highly evolved than they are. We got better ideas. And it's our fucking turn. SCUM will not be collateral damage. We will not be the corpses they feed on. We're gonna grab back what's rightfully ours. *(to* **Nico***)* C'mon!

Nico Come where?

Valerie We're gonna go to The Factory, OK? Make Warhol give me my script back.

Nico I am not coming with you to the...

Valerie *pulls a gun from the brown paper bag.*

Valerie I'll level with you. I bought a gun. Two guns: there's a .32 Beretta in here as well.

Nico Please do not shoot me.

Valerie Look, Christa—you need to choose. Are you a weak little Daddy's Girl? Or are you with me? Well, are you?

Pause

Nico No.

Valerie Excuse me?

Nico I must stand alone.

Valerie SCUM needs you.

Nico The Society For Cutting Up Men. And yet, you are holding a gun to *my* head.

Pause. **Valerie** *lowers the gun.*

The idea of you hurting anybody is a fantasy.

Valerie It used to be. The Manifesto was a parody. To make people laugh, so they'd listen!

Nico I am listening.

Valerie It isn't funny anymore. If I don't even own my own words, I have nothing.

Nico I can feel how much pain you are in, and I will help you.

Valerie You promise?

Nico You will write more: words that will change the world.

Valerie You really believe that?

Nico But not with that *(the gun)* in your hand. Come on.

Nico *tentatively reaches for the gun.*

Valerie Something else you can take?

Valerie *points the gun straight at her.*

Nice try.

Nico *retreats.*

You don't need hidden cameras. You've been here all along. Haven't you, Andy?

Nico Andy?

Valerie Like you said: you're in drag.

Onscreen: the images of Nazi soldiers and ideal women begin to burn.

Nico Why are you calling me Andy?

Valerie Yeah: you're listening. You've been listening all day! You son of a bitch. You've been sucking up all my ideas.

Nico I am not Andy!

Valerie You're garbage! The ultimate phoney! But you said one true thing. You can't just rant about what's wrong. It's time for SCUM to commit a definitive act.

The phone rings. Pause. Tentatively, **Nico** *moves to it and picks up the receiver. She adopts the same fey 'Warhol' pose as before, and turns her back on* **Valerie.** *A light change throws* **Nico** *in to silhouette.* **Valerie** *trains the gun on her.*

Andy: do not turn your back on me!

Nico, *as Warhol, waves her hand at* **Valerie**: *'wait'.*

Nico *(on phone, as Warhol)* Oh hey, Viva!

Valerie Do not ignore me, Andy.

Nico *(on phone, as Warhol)* Really? You're getting it coloured?

Valerie Look at me.

Nico *(on phone, as Warhol)* Well, red would look great. Like Rita Hayworth.

Valerie *cocks the gun.*

Valerie Why'd you steal my script?

Nico *(on phone, as Warhol)* It could be sooo glamorous.

Valerie You should know better! You know that words matter!

Valerie *fires her gun.* **Nico**/*Warhol lowers the phone in slow motion.*

MY words matter!

Valerie *fires a second time.*

OUR words matter and not you not anyone is going to steal from us ever again—because WE are SCUM! We are female revolution! Your time is up!

Valerie *fires a third time.*

Blackout.

FINALE:

Onscreen: archive footage of the arrest of the real Valerie Solanas. On stage: flashbulbs pop. **Valerie** *poses for pictures. Flashbulbs stop.*

Onscreen: a caption '1986', 'Free University, Berlin' appears on the screen in a white eighties font.

A light snaps up on **Nico** *at the stage left mic.*

Nico *(to audience)* Hello Berlin. Every time I return to this city, I remember why I left. I liked it best when it was burning.

Valerie *(to audience)* Hi again. I want to say something. Shooting Andy Warhol was a moral act.

Nico Total destruction is…the most beautiful thing I have ever seen.

Valerie I consider it immoral that he survived. I should have done target practice.

Nico You know, a bomb blast takes time to be felt. First comes the flash, then the shock waves—and only then do the buildings fall…

Valerie That would be my final message. Do target practice!

An electronic soundtrack starts. Images of key feminist moments from 1986-2018 are montaged in the manner of an 80s music video as **Nico** *sings her own song 'Win a Few', its final refrain in German.*

Lights snap off.

EPILOGUE:

*Onscreen captions: 'New York', 'The Chelsea Hotel', '2018'. Lights snap up on **Valerie**, waiting on the balcony, observing people below, the sound of traffic somehow more present as **Nico** enters.*

Nico Valerie.

Valerie Hey. Didn't know if you'd show.

Nico My diary is...less full these days. What has happened to The Chelsea?

Valerie Closed for renovations. Technically, we're trespassing.

Nico Nobody can see us, right?

Valerie Only cats. And the truly wasted.

Beat.

Nico How have you been?

Valerie Dead. You?

Nico Long dead. How?

Valerie I don't wanna talk about it.

Nico It is upsetting?

Valerie It's freakin' embarrassing. *(beat)* Overdose.

Nico So why am I here?

Valerie Look down there *(points to the street)* Women are marching. Finally! *(reading a banner)* 'Girls just want to have fundamental human rights.'

Nico *(beat)* I must tell you... I did finally read your Manifesto.

Valerie Yeah? What'd you think?

Nico It disturbs me. For all your claims that women don't need men... it is all about men. Men do this, the male is that... And now you are famous for shooting a more famous man.

Valerie Would you have read my Manifesto if I hadn't?

Nico I want to know one thing. That day: did you always mean to shoot Andy?

Valerie I just wanted my script back.

Nico It was not really about a script.

Valerie I came up with him in the elevator: he was friendly. I thought, you know: perhaps we can figure this out. But then we walk in to the Factory and somebody hands him a phone and he waves his hand at me to wait. While he gossips.

Nico He was like that. It was nothing personal.

Valerie If somebody thinks you don't matter, because you're female, or poor—or just because you're *you*—that's personal.

Nico You still cannot rest?

Beat.

Valerie What about you? How...?

Nico Brain haemorrhage. Whilst cycling. Alone.

Valerie Where have you, um, ended up?

Nico Not Berlin.

Valerie Good.

Nico You?

Valerie Still here.

Nico You chose to stay?

Valerie I'm waiting.

Nico For what?

Valerie A female society. It's coming, I figure it'll only take another fifty years.

Nico I think you should give it one hundred.

Valerie Jeez—really?! Wanna keep me company?

Nico Oh... You know.

Valerie Places to be, things to do...

Nico I do not want to. You tried to murder my friend.

Beat.

Valerie Look at that. You learned not to bullshit.

Nico Yes.

Valerie Was he really a friend?

Nico *(beat)* After I went solo, I didn't see him for years. I tried to meet him in New York, in the eighties. But he didn't want to know me once I got 'fat" and 'ugly'. Hardly any of the old crowd did.

Valerie You don't look too upset.

Nico I never wanted people to touch my bottom. I wanted to touch their souls.

Valerie Maybe you're SCUM after all.

Nico There was...something in your Manifesto that struck a chord. I made five more solo albums. But in record shops, I could never find them. They were always filed under 'V' for Velvet Underground. But Lou Reed's were always under 'R'.

Valerie Hey. Stop ranting about men.

Beat. **Nico** *smiles.*

They're not relevant at this point. It's what the women are gonna do.

Valerie *addresses the audience.*

So what are we going to do?

Nico Who are you talking to?

Valerie OK: I'll level with you. This isn't really the Chelsea Hotel. It's London, 2019.

Light change to reveal audience (orchestrated by **Valerie***).*

Nico I hate London! I did the worst gig of my life at The Fridge!

Valerie This isn't The Fridge. And these people: I think they really get it. *(to audience member)* 'Lucy'? 'Jeff'? Meet Christa. Christa—'Jeff', 'Lucy'.

Nico *(pause)* Hi.

Valerie I've had a lot of time to think and—I hate to admit it—but killing all the men isn't going to work. Men aren't the target: it's the system they've created. How do we take that out? Any thoughts? 'Lucy'? *(responds to whatever it is, or prompts her, moving on if nothing is suggested)* 'Jeff'? Everyone needs to help with this! We're gonna pool all our ideas and make a new Manifesto. *(beat)* All of you: think for a moment. What could we do? *(lets them think for a few seconds)* Hey: if you think of something later, let us know. And then make it happen, whatever it is. I dare you! Cos I'm dead. It's all on you!

Nico If it's all on them, why don't you move on?

Valerie Where to?

Nico It's a big universe. Its door is open...

Nico goes to move off.

Valerie Oh hey: I nearly forgot.

Valerie produces two bottles of Budweiser.

It's not German.

Nico *takes one of the beers, swigs down nearly all of her beer in one gulp.*
Valerie *takes a swig from her own bottle and raises her bottle.*

Valerie To conceited, kooky, funky females, grooving off each other, cracking each other up whilst cracking open the universe!

Beat.

Nico To the universe.

Nico *and* **Valerie** *raise their bottles in a toast to the audience* as *#TimesUp flashes across their faces, then blackout as a contemporary remix of 'All Tomorrow's Parties' plays.*

Lights up. The performers bow and exit. Only a spotlight is left on a gun atop the Brillo boxes. Legend onscreen #SCUM2019

END.

Acknowledgements

With thanks to:

Holly Kendrick, Tania Harrison, Wilton's Music Hall,
Latitude Festival, Women at RADA, Jules Deering, Justin David,
Dr J, Tessa Garland, Darren Evans, Clarisse M Kye,
Sanna-Karina Aab, Cockpit Theatre, Lisa Goldman, Chris Rolls,
Sue Parrish, Marie McCarthy, Nick Neighem, Anton Binder,
Khobir Wiseman-Goldstein, Zoe Harvey, Judith Hibberd,
Lynn Wiseman

Polly Wiseman, 2019

Also from Inkandescent

SWANSONG
by Nathan Evans

A gentleman called Joan lands in a subdued, suburban care home like a colourful, combustible cocktail. A veteran of Gay Lib, he dons battle dress and seeks an ally in the young, gay but disappointingly conventional care assistant Craig for his assault on the heteronormativity of the care system. Then, in this most unlikely of settings, Joan is offered love by a gentleman called Jim...

This bittersweet comedy explores issues surrounding care and LGBT elders. It premiered at the Royal Vauxhall Tavern, London on 17 October 2018, presented by 89th Productions as part of And What? Queer Arts Festival.

'Side-splittingly funny and achingly romantic.
A play about ageing disgracefully that's ferociously full of life.'
RIKKI BEADLE-BLAIR

Also from Inkandescent

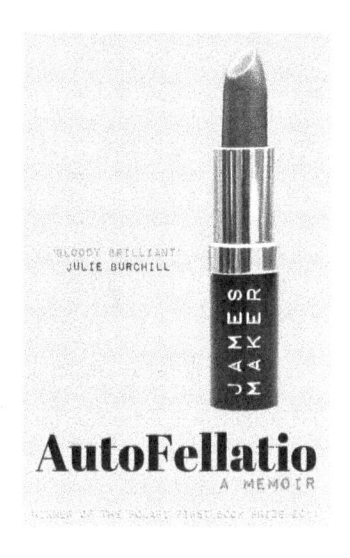

AutoFellatio
by James Maker

Apart from herpes and Lulu—everything is eventually swept away

According to Wikipedia, only a few men can actually perform the act of autofellatio. We never discover whether James Maker—from rock bands Raymonde and RPLA—is one of them. But certainly, as a story-teller and raconteur, he is one in a million.

From Bermondsey enfant terrible to Valencian grande dame—a journey that variously stops off at Morrissey Confidant, Glam Rock Star, Dominatrix, Actor and Restoration Man—his long and winding tale is a compendium of memorable bons mots woven into a patchwork quilt of heart-warming anecdotes that make you feel like you've hit the wedding-reception jackpot by being unexpectedly seated next the groom's witty homosexual uncle.

More about the music industry than about coming out, this remix is a refreshing reminder that much of what we now think of as post-punk British rock and pop, owes much to the generation of musicians like James. The only criticism here is that—as in life—fellatio ultimately cums to an end.

'a glam-rock Naked Civil Servant in court shoes. But funnier. And tougher'
MARK SIMPSON

Also from Inkandescent

THREADS
by Nathan Evans & Justin David

If Alice landed in London not Wonderland this book might be the result. Threads is the first collection from Nathan Evans, each poem complemented by a bespoke photograph from Justin David and, like Tenniel's illustrations for Carroll, picture and word weft and warp to create an alchemic (rabbit) whole.

On one page, the image of an alien costume, hanging surreally beside a school uniform on a washing line, accompanies a poem about fleeing suburbia. On another, a poem about seeking asylum accompanies the image of another displaced alien on an urban train. Spun from heartfelt emotion and embroidered with humour, Threads will leave you aching with longing and laughter.

'In this bright and beautiful collaboration, poetry and photography join hands, creating sharp new ways to picture our lives and loves.'
NEIL BARTLETT

Also from Inkandescent

He's Done Ever So Well For Himself
by Justin David

As a little boy, growing up in the half of the country decimated by the harsh economics of Mrs Thatcher, Jamie dreams of rubbing shoulders with the glamorous creatures from the pages of *Smash Hits* – only to discover years later that once amongst them, the real stars in his life are the ones he left behind.

Not least, his mother Gloria whose one-liners and put-downs are at as colourful as her pink furry mules and DayGlo orange dungarees. All of this, she carries off with the panache of a television landlady.

Jamie swaps the high heels and high hair of 80s Midlands for the high expectations of London at the heart of 90s Cool Britannia. He's drawn towards a new family of misfits, fuelled by drugs and sexual experimentation – from which he must ultimately untangle himself in order to fulfil his dreams. This bitingly funny tale of conflict and self-discovery is *page-turning friction.*

'For anyone who's lived and loved and fought to be the person they're meant to be'
MATT CAIN

inkandescent

Inkandescent Publishing was created in 2016 by Justin David and Nathan Evans to shine a light on diverse and distinctive voices.

Sign up to our mailing list to stay informed about future releases:

www.inkandescent.co.uk

Follow us on Facebook:

@InkandescentPublishing

and on Twitter:

@InkandescentUK